How To Use This Study Guide

This five-lesson study guide corresponds to *"Questions and Answers With Rick Renner 2025"* (**Renner TV**). Each lesson in this study guide covers a topic that is addressed during the program series, with questions and references supplied to draw you deeper into your own private study of the Scriptures on this subject.

To derive the most benefit from this study guide, consider the following:

First, watch or listen to the program prior to working through the corresponding lesson in this guide. (Programs can also be viewed at **renner.org** by clicking on the Media/Archives links or on our Renner Ministries YouTube channel.)

Second, take the time to look up the scriptures included in each lesson. Prayerfully consider their application to your own life.

Third, use a journal or notebook to make note of your answers to each lesson's Study Questions and Practical Application challenges.

Fourth, invest specific time in prayer and in the Word of God to consult with the Holy Spirit. Write down the scriptures or insights He reveals to you.

Finally, take action! Whatever the Lord tells you to do according to His Word, do it.

For added insights on this subject, it is recommended that you obtain Rick Renner's books *A Life Ablaze, Dressed To Kill, Apostles and Prophets*, and *How To Keep Your Head on Straight in a World Gone Crazy*, as well as Denise Renner's book *Jesus Is Your Healer* and Mike Clark's book *There's a Light at the End of Your Tunnel.* You may also select from Rick's other available resources by placing your order at **renner.org** or by calling 1-800-742-5593.

TOPIC

Who Is Holding Back the Beast?

SCRIPTURES

1. **2 Thessalonians 2:2** — That ye be not soon shaken in mind, or be troubled, neither by spirit, nor by word, nor by letter as from us, as that the day of Christ is at hand.

2. **2 Thessalonians 2:2** (*RIV*) — Some things will be happening right before His coming that could shake you up quite a bit. I'm referring to events that will be so dramatic that they could leave your head spinning — occurrences of such a serious nature that many people will end up feeling alarmed, panicked, intimidated, and unnerved. Naturally speaking, these events could nearly drive you over the brink emotionally, putting your nerves on edge and making you feel apprehensive and insecure. I wish I could tell you these incidents were just going to be a one-shot deal, but when they finally get rolling, they're going to keep coming and coming, one right after another. That's why you have to determine not to be shaken or moved by anything you see or hear. You need to get a grip on your mind and refuse to allow yourself to be traumatized by these events. If you let these things get to you, it won't be too long until you're a nervous wreck! That's why you have to decide beforehand that you're not going to give in and allow fright to penetrate its way into your mind and emotions until it runs your whole life.

3. **2 Thessalonians 2:3** — Let no man deceive you by any means: for that day shall not come, except there come a falling away first, and that man of sin be revealed, the son of perdition.

4. **2 Thessalonians 2:3** (*RIV*) — In light of these things, I urge you to refuse to allow anyone to take advantage of you. For example, you won't need a letter to tell you when the day of the Lord has come. You ought to know by now that this day can't come until first a worldwide insurgency, rebellion, riot, and mutiny against God has come about in society. Once that occurs, the world will then be primed, prepared, and ready to embrace the Man of Lawlessness.

A Note From Rick Renner

I am on a personal quest to see a "revival of the Bible" so people can establish their lives on a firm foundation that will stand strong and endure the test as end-time storm winds begin to intensify.

In order to experience a revival of the Bible in your personal life, it is important to take time each day to read, receive, and apply its truths to your life. James tells us that if we will continue in the perfect law of liberty — refusing to be forgetful hearers, but determined to be doers — we will be blessed in our ways. As you watch or listen to the programs in this series and work through this corresponding study guide, I trust you will search the Scriptures and allow the Holy Spirit to help you hear something new from God's Word that applies specifically to your life. I encourage you to be a doer of the Word He reveals to you. Whatever the cost, I assure you — it will be worth it.

> Thy words were found, and I did eat them;
> and thy word was unto me the joy and rejoicing of mine heart:
> for I am called by thy name, O Lord God of hosts.
> — Jeremiah 15:16

Your brother and friend in Jesus Christ,

Rick Renner

Unless otherwise indicated, all scripture quotations are taken from the *King James Version* of the Bible.

Scripture quotations marked (*AMP*) are taken from the *Amplified*® *Bible*, copyright © 2015 by The Lockman Foundation, La Habra, CA 90631. All rights reserved.

Scripture quotations marked (*AMPC*) are taken from the *Amplified*® *Bible, Classic Edition*. Copyright © 1954, 1958, 1962, 1964, 1965, 1987 by The Lockman Foundation. Used by permission. **www.Lockman.org**.

Scripture quotations marked (*NKJV*) are taken from the *New King James Version*®. Copyright © 1982 by Thomas Nelson. Used by permission. All rights reserved.

Scripture quotations marked (*NLT*) are taken from the Holy Bible, *New Living Translation*, copyright © 1996, 2004, 2015 by Tyndale House Foundation. Used by permission of Tyndale House Publishers, Inc., Carol Stream, Illinois 60188. All rights reserved.

Scriptures quoted from the Renner Interpretive Version ® (*RIV*) copyrighted © 2020, 2024 by Teaching You Can Trust, LLC, and published by Harrison House Publishers. Used by permission. Renner.org. Harrisonhouse.com.

Questions and Answers With Rick Renner 2025

Copyright © 2025 by Teaching You Can Trust, LLC
1814 W. Tacoma St.
Broken Arrow, OK 74012-1406

Published by Rick Renner Ministries
www.renner.org

ISBN 13: 978-1-6675-1470-3

ISBN 13 eBook: 978-1-6675-1471-0

All rights reserved. No portion of this book may be reproduced or transmitted in any form or by any means — electronic, mechanical, photocopy, recording, scanning, or other — except for brief quotations in critical reviews or articles, without the prior written permission of the Publisher.

5. **2 Thessalonians 2:6** — And now ye know what withholdeth that he might be revealed in his time.

6. **2 Thessalonians 2:7** — For the mystery of iniquity doth already work: only he who now letteth will let, until he be taken out of the way.

7. **2 Thessalonians 2:8** — And then shall that Wicked be revealed, whom the Lord shall consume with the spirit of his mouth, and shall destroy with the brightness of his coming.

8. **2 Thessalonians 2:6** (*RIV*) — Now in light of everything I've told you before, you ought to be well aware by now that there is a supernatural force at work preventing the materialization of this person and the disclosure of his identity. This retraining force I'm referring to is so strong that it's currently putting on the brakes and holding back the unveiling of this wicked person, stalling and postponing his manifestation. But when the right moment comes, this evil one will no longer be withheld, and he will emerge on the world scene! The screen that has been hiding his true identity and guarding him from world view will suddenly be pulled back and evaporate — and he will step out on center stage to let everyone know who he is.

GREEK WORDS

1. "falling away" — **ἀποστασία** (*apostasia*): where we get the English word apostasy; a compound of the words **ἀπό** (*apo*), which means away, and the word **ἵστημι** (*histemi*), meaning to stand; compounded together, it literally means one that steps away from something; used historically to describe a defection, a rebellion, or a mutiny

2. "sin" — **ἀνομία** (*anomia*): lawlessness; without law; a law-less attitude.

3. "withholdeth" or "letteth" — **κατέχω** (*katecho*): a compound of the word **κατά** (*kata*), meaning down, and the word **ἔχω** (*echo*), which means to hold; it means to hold against, to restrain, to postpone, to oppose, to stall, or to put on the brakes

4. "revealed" — **ἀποκαλύπτω** (*apokalupto*): a compound of the words **ἀπό** (*apo*), meaning away, and **καλύπτω** (*kalupto*), which means to veil; as the word **ἀποκαλύπτω** (*apokalupto*) in this verse, it means that in that precise moment when the church is removed, or in that very moment when the church is evacuated — and not until then — the curtains are going to be pulled back and the wicked one is going to appear center stage

SYNOPSIS

The five lessons in this study titled *Questions and Answers With Rick Renner 2025* will focus on the following topics:

- Who Is Holding Back the Beast?
- Is God Guiding Your Next Step?
- Why Hasn't Your Healing Arrived?
- How Do You Walk in Authority?
- What Issues Are Worth Debating?

The emphasis of this lesson:

Uncertainty about the end times often stirs up fear in people's minds, but God's Word brings clarity and peace to this subject. In this lesson, Rick explains what rebellion Paul was referring to in Second Thessalonians 2:3; who the Restrainer is; and when the Antichrist will be revealed. By looking carefully at the original Greek text, we learn that as believers, we need not be troubled. Instead, we can stand firm on Scripture and encourage one another with hope.

'Be Not Soon Shaken in Mind'

Questions about the end times are not uncommon in both the wider world and among believers. And unfortunately, topics like the Rapture, the Second Coming, and the Tribulation have commonly stirred fear and confusion in people's hearts and minds, even dating back to Paul's time. For example, the church in Thessalonica was mistakenly told that the Rapture had already occurred and that they had missed it. This produced great distress among the Thessalonian believers. Imagine the fear of believing you'd been left behind in the Rapture!

Such misunderstandings still occur today, and many people feel anxious when contemplating the end times. Even Rick Renner shared that, as a child, he was terrified of the Rapture. Much of this fear, however, stems from a lack of understanding or uncertainty surrounding this topic.

But here's the good news: There's no need to be afraid. In fact, Paul wrote to the Thessalonian believers to reassure them of this very truth:

That ye be not soon shaken in mind, or be troubled, neither by spirit, nor by word, nor by letter as from us, as that the day of Christ is at hand.

— 2 Thessalonians 2:2

Although Paul was addressing the Thessalonian believers, his message still applies to us today. We don't need to fear the subject of the end times! As believers, we are encouraged to "comfort one another with these words" (*see* 1 Thessalonians 4:18). If you find yourself anxious or fearful about the Rapture or other end-time events, consider reading Rick's book *The Rapture, the Antichrist, and the Tribulation — An End-Times Countdown and What Happens Next*. He wrote this book to help settle confusion and bring peace to those struggling with fear regarding these topics.

To help better explain this, Rick offered a fresh interpretation of Second Thessalonians 2:2 in the program. The *Renner Interpretive Version* (*RIV*) is a conceptual interpretation of the New Testament that draws on the concepts in the original Greek language and brings them into the text in a clear, contemporary way. Here is the *RIV* rendering of this verse:

Some things will be happening right before His coming that could shake you up quite a bit. I'm referring to events that will be so dramatic that they could leave your head spinning — occurrences of such a serious nature that many people will end up feeling alarmed, panicked, intimidated, and unnerved. Naturally speaking, these events could nearly drive you over the brink emotionally, putting your nerves on edge and making you feel apprehensive and insecure. I wish I could tell you these incidents were just going to be a one-shot deal, but when they finally get rolling, they're going to keep coming and coming, one right after another. That's why you have to determine not to be shaken or moved by anything you see or hear. You need to get a grip on your mind and refuse to allow yourself to be traumatized by these events. If you let these things get to you, it won't be too long until you're a nervous wreck! That's why you have to decide beforehand that you're not going to give in and allow fright to penetrate its way into your mind and emotions until it runs your whole life.

Second Thessalonians 2:2 speaks directly to the challenges we face today. Just a quick look on YouTube reveals that there are countless fear- and panic-driven messages circulating online. People say all kinds of extreme or misleading things just to get clicks or views, which only fuels anxiety and puts people into a state of fear. But, remember, Paul clearly taught we are "not [to be] soon shaken in mind, or be troubled, neither by spirit, nor by word, nor by letter as from us, as that the day of Christ is at hand" (2 Thessalonians 2:2).

From the earliest days of the Church, people have been panic-stricken about the Rapture and other end-time events. But understanding what the Bible truly teaches removes all fear and panic. When we ground ourselves in Scripture and seek clarity, we will discover God's all-surpassing peace (*see* Philippians 4:7).

Now that we've laid some groundwork, let's begin with question one.

Question One: What is the rebellion spoken of in Second Thessalonians 2:3?

When it comes to the end times, certain words and phrases in Scripture can spark big questions. One such phrase appears in Second Thessalonians 2:3, where Paul spoke of "the rebellion" — or, as the *King James Version* renders it, the "falling away." But what exactly is this "rebellion"? Is it a political uprising, a spiritual departure, the Rapture, or something else entirely?

Before we explore this further, let's take a look at what Second Thessalonians 2:3 says:

> **Let no man deceive you by any means: for that day shall not come, except there come a falling away first, and that man of sin be revealed, the son of perdition.**

Some claim that the word "rebellion" (written in the *King James Version* as "falling away") refers to the Rapture — the Church departing from the world to meet Jesus in the air. But this is not the case. When studying a passage like this, it's essential to examine how the words were used historically in context.

The phrase "falling away" comes from the Greek word *apostasia*, which is where we get the English word "apostasy." This term is a compound of the words *apo*, which means *away*, and the word *histemi*, meaning *to stand*. Together, they paint the picture of *one who steps away from something* and were historically used to describe *a defection, a rebellion,* or *a mutiny*. This Greek word was never used in a positive sense.

Paul, a linguist, chose the word *apostasia* here very intentionally. He was not describing the Rapture of the Church, but rather a departure from the faith. The same warning appears in First Timothy 4:1, which says, "…in the latter times *some shall depart from the faith*…." Paul was referring to a worldwide mutiny that will occur against God at the close of the age.

In the Greek text of Second Thessalonians 2:3, the words "falling away" are preceded by a definite article — *the* falling away — indicating a very specific, unprecedented event. Yes, Church history has seen many defections from the faith, but Paul was pointing to one decisive, massive departure that will occur just before the Antichrist is revealed.

In this passage, the Antichrist is called "that man of sin." The word "sin" here is the Greek word *anomia*, meaning *lawlessness, without law*, or *a lawless attitude*. A more accurate rendering of this word would be "the man of lawlessness." Such a figure can only rise in a world already steeped in lawlessness. Not just in terms of chaos in the streets — although that may be part of it — but a worldwide rejection of God's Law. Society will declare, "We've moved on. We've outgrown those old morals and beliefs," and reject the teachings of the Bible.

A new world order will emerge with its own ethics, its own rules, and no regard for God's standards. And when *the* great falling away has taken place, the stage will be set for humanity to welcome the man of lawlessness — the Antichrist.

Taking the original Greek meaning of the key words in these verses into account, the *Renner Interpretive Version* (*RIV*) reads:

> **In light of these things, I urge you to refuse to allow anyone to take advantage of you. For example, you won't need a letter to tell you when the day of the Lord has come. You ought to know by now that this day can't come until first a worldwide insurgency, rebellion, riot, and mutiny against God has come about in society. Once that occurs, the world will then be primed, prepared, and ready to embrace the Man of Lawlessness.**

So when the Bible speaks of "the rebellion" in Second Thessalonians 2:3, it is foretelling of a time when society at large will abandon the authority of God's Word and the moral foundation of Judeo-Christian ethics. This deliberate departure will help pave the way for the Antichrist.

Question Two: Who is the Restrainer in Scripture, or do we know?

In the same passage in which Paul warned of the great falling away, he also introduced another mysterious element tied to the end-times timeline. He wrote of a force — whether a person, power, or presence — that is actively holding back the rise of lawlessness and the revealing of the "man of sin." This force, often referred to as "the Restrainer," is not named directly by Paul, leaving believers to wonder who or what it might be. Second Thessalonians 2:6 says:

> **And now ye know what withholdeth that he [the Antichrist] might be revealed in his time.**

Notice the phrase "in his time." The Antichrist cannot be revealed until his appointed moment. According to this verse, something — or someone — is holding him back, postponing his unveiling, and restraining him until the precise time comes when he can (and will) be revealed.

In verse 7, Paul continued:

> **For the mystery of iniquity doth already work: only he who now letteth will let, until he be taken out of the way.**

The words "letteth will let" are derived from the same Greek word translated as "withholdeth" in verse 6 — the word *katecho*. This word is made up of two words: the word *kata*, which means down, and the word *echo*, meaning *to hold*. When you put these two words together, it means *to hold against, to restrain, to postpone, to oppose, to stall,* or *to put on the brakes.* In other words, Paul was describing an active force in the world right now that is holding back evil. But the question remains: Who — or what — is the Restrainer?

Throughout 2,000 years of Church history, various ideas have been proposed as possible answers to this question. The earliest believers thought it was the Roman Senate. Their reasoning was simple: without the Senate's stabilizing influence, power-hungry emperors could have plunged the empire into chaos. They thought, "If we didn't have a senate, there is no telling what these crazy emperors would do." Those early believers genuinely believed the Roman Senate was the Restrainer holding back evil. However, the Roman Senate disappeared centuries ago, so this theory is no longer valid.

Others have suggested Michael the Archangel is the Restrainer. In Daniel 10, Michael is seen disputing with Satan over the body of Moses, leading some to conclude he must be the one holding back evil. Alternately, another view is that the preaching of the Gospel itself is the restraining force. But Scripture tells us that the preaching of the Gospel continues even during the Tribulation (*see* Revelation 7:4; 14:6), so it can't be the Great Restrainer.

Still others have claimed that the Holy Spirit is the Restrainer, who will one day be taken from the earth. But this can't be the case either — because no one can be saved without the Holy Spirit's work in their heart, and we know that during the Tribulation, countless people will come to Christ.

When we come to verse 7, we read, "…Only he who now letteth will let, *until he be taken out of the way.*" In Greek, this phrase literally says, "…Until he is removed from the middle of everything." Knowing this, immediately we can rule out several possibilities. The Holy Spirit will never be removed from the earth — because His presence is essential for salvation, so He is not the Restrainer. Michael the Archangel will not be removed, so he is not the Restrainer either. The preaching of the Gospel also will not be removed from the earth. So who *can* be removed from "the middle of everything" — and who is already everywhere? The answer is: the Church.

The Body of Christ is in every sphere of life: the entertainment industry, the judicial system, the educational arena, government, business, science — you name it. Wherever you go in the world, you will find believers. In the program, Rick shared a story about going to the gym in Moscow and being greeted by someone who said, "Pastor Rick, I go to your church." Encounters like that are a reminder: the Church is everywhere.

But a day is coming when the Restrainer — that's us, the Church — will be taken out of the midst of everything. In an instant, we'll disappear from the world scene. Paul described this event in First Thessalonians 4:17-18, when believers will be "caught up" to meet the Lord in the air. And according to Second Thessalonians 2, that removal will be the very moment the Antichrist is revealed. How do we know this? Paul wrote in verse 8:

> **And then shall that Wicked be revealed, whom the Lord shall consume with the spirit of his mouth, and shall destroy with the brightness of his coming.**
> **— 2 Thessalonians 2:8**

The Greek text says, "Then — in that precise moment — the Wicked One shall be revealed." The definite article shows Paul wasn't speaking of just any wicked man, but *the* Wicked One — the Antichrist. The word "revealed" is also significant. In Greek it is a form of *apokalupto*, a compound of two words: the word *apo* meaning *away* and *kalupto*, which means *to veil*. As a compound, the word *apokalupto* means *in that precise moment* or *in that very moment*. In this verse, it pictures a veil suddenly being pulled away so that the identity of the Antichrist is fully exposed.

Taking into account all the original Greek meanings of these key words, the *Renner Interpretive Version* of Second Thessalonians 2:6-7 reads:

> **Now in light of everything I've told you before, you ought to be well aware by now that there is a supernatural force at work preventing the materialization of this person and the disclosure of his identity. This restraining force I'm referring to is so strong that it's currently putting on the brakes and holding back the unveiling of this wicked person, stalling and postponing his manifestation. But when the right moment comes, this evil one will no longer be withheld, and he will emerge on the world scene! The screen that has been hiding his true identity and guarding him from world view will suddenly be pulled back and evaporate — and he will step out on center stage to let everyone know who he is.**

So who is the Great Restrainer? Scripture points to the Church. When the Church is removed, the brakes will be off, and the man of lawlessness will have his moment on the stage of history.

Question Three: Will Christians be around when the Antichrist appears, and will we be able to recognize him?

Paul's words make it clear that the Antichrist can't be revealed until the Restrainer is taken out of the way. That naturally leads us to an important question many believers wrestle with: Will believers still be on the earth when the Antichrist finally appears? And if so, will they be able to recognize him?

Since the Church is the Restrainer, we know that according to Second Thessalonians 2:8 we will not be present when the Antichrist is revealed. First, the Church will be caught up in the Rapture to be united with the Lord Jesus in the air, and then, Paul wrote, "shall that Wicked be revealed"

(2 Thessalonians 2:8). It is only after the Great Restrainer is removed that the Antichrist will be revealed and his nefarious activities will unfold, including the enforcement of the mark of the beast (*see* Revelation 13:16-18).

This verse clearly shows us why we don't need to live in fear. You don't need to be concerned with when the Antichrist will appear or when the mark of the beast will come. Scripture tells us the mark of the beast can't appear until after the Church is gone. That means if you belong to Christ and you are an authentic Christian, you don't have to worry about accidentally receiving it. You won't even be here when that time comes.

This is the power of sound teaching: it doesn't stir up anxiety but, instead, settles the heart with God's peace and truth. Rather than worrying or fretting, we can rest in the assurance that God's Word is true, and it has a lot to say about these end-time events.

In the next lesson, we'll turn from the subject of the end-times to examine questions related to God's guidance.

STUDY QUESTIONS

Study to shew thyself approved unto God, a workman that needeth not to be ashamed, rightly dividing the word of truth.
— 2 Timothy 2:15

1. Take a moment to reread the *Renner Interpretive Version* of Second Thessalonians 2:2. How does this interpretation expand your understanding of Paul's warning not to be "shaken in mind" or "troubled"? Read First Thessalonians 4:18. How should believers respond to one another when talking about the Rapture and the end times?

2. Why is it important to compare popular teachings, media claims, or cultural speculation about the end times with the Word of God?

3. Who or what is the "Restrainer" in Second Thessalonians 2:7 that must be taken out of the way? Before this lesson, did you know the identity of the Restrainer?

4. According to Paul in Second Thessalonians 2, what must happen before the Antichrist can be revealed? At what point will the Antichrist begin carrying out his nefarious activities, including requiring the taking of the mark of the beast?

PRACTICAL APPLICATION

But be ye doers of the word, and not hearers only,
deceiving your own selves.
— James 1:22

1. Paul reminded us in Second Thessalonians 2 that the Church will not be present for the revealing of the Antichrist. How does this assurance change the way you respond to alarming news reports or world events today? What specific scriptures can you hold on to when fear or confusion about the end times begins to rise? Consider First Thessalonians 4:18 and John 14:27.

2. Instead of worrying about the Antichrist and his actions, where should believers keep their focus? When friends, family, or other believers are anxious about "the mark of the beast" or end-time speculation, how might you use the passage we've studied in Second Thessalonians 2 to gently encourage them with truth and peace?

3. Take time this week to thank God for the peace He gives through His Word and Philippians 4:6-7. Pray for the Holy Spirit's help to not only experience that peace personally but also to share it with others who may be troubled by fears about the future.

LESSON 2

TOPIC

Is God Guiding Your Next Step?

SCRIPTURES

1. **James 1:4** — But let patience have her perfect work, that ye may be perfect and entire, wanting nothing.

2. **James 1:4** (*RIV*) — But you're the one who must make the choice to let this God-given endurance do its work. And if you'll let endurance run its full course, it will advance you into higher levels of spiritual maturity. Choosing to let endurance run its full course takes work — but if you'll stick with this process all the way to the end, you'll advance to high spiritual levels in your life....

GREEK WORDS

1. "patience" — ὑπομονή (*hupomone*): a compound of the word ὑπὸ (*hupo*) and the word μένω (*meno*); the word ὑπὸ (*hupo*) means to be under, as if to be under a heavy load; the word μένω (*meno*) describes one who says, "I'm staying in this spot and I'm not moving," and means to abide or to be fixed and unmoving; compounded, the word ὑπομονή (*hupomone*) describes a person under a heavy, heavy load who has resolved, "I'm not moving no matter how hard it gets"; used in a military sense to describe soldiers who stuck it out and maintained their territory; hang-in-there power

SYNOPSIS

Faith often requires patience, discernment, and obedience — even when God's promises seem delayed. In this lesson, Rick addresses five key questions about moving forward in faith, recognizing God's timing, avoiding missteps, stepping out in peace, and remaining faithful in the small things. Through biblical examples in Abraham's life and through Rick's own experiences, we will learn how to persevere, grow into God's promises, and take steps of faith with confidence, knowing that God's plan will unfold in the right season.

The emphasis of this lesson:

God calls each believer to walk in patient, obedient faith. Even when answers seem delayed, mistakes are made, or challenges arise in our lives, God equips us to discern His will, boldly step into it, and faithfully grow into receiving the promises He has given to us. By trusting His timing, listening for His guidance, and remaining faithful in small beginnings, we can see God's plans come to pass and experience the fullness of what He has promised.

Question One: When you are believing and trusting God for something in your life and it hasn't come to pass yet, how do you know whether it's just not the right time or it's the enemy coming against you?

In the last lesson, we saw how God's Word gives peace in the midst of end-time uncertainty. But what about the uncertainties we face in our daily walk of faith? Every believer, at some point, wrestles with questions like: *Why hasn't my prayer been answered yet? Is it God's timing, or is the enemy resisting me?* These are not small questions — they touch the core of our trust in God. And these questions are not new — even the earliest believers wrestled with them. Let's turn to Scripture to see how James comforted believers who faced the same struggles.

In his letter, James wrote to Christians who were discouraged by long delays in their prayers, and he gave them this encouragement:

> **But let patience have her perfect work, that ye may be perfect and entire, wanting nothing.**
>
> **—James 1:4**

When you're going through intense struggles in life, it can be hard to wait. No one likes waiting for answers to their prayers, requests, and petitions from God, but patience is important. If we look at the Greek word for patience in this verse, it is *hupomone*, which is a compound of two words: the word *hupo* and *meno*.

The word *hupo* means *to be under*, as if under a heavy load. The word *meno* means *to remain, to abide*, or *to stay put*. It pictures a firm resolution: *This is my place, and I'm not moving*. It's the same word Jesus used in John 15:7 when He said, "If ye *abide* in me, and my words *abide* in you…." Both instances of "abide" are the word *meno*. It is essentially saying, "If My Word is fixed in you and unmoving, and if you are fixed in Me and unmoving…."

So when you compound the word *meno* with the prefix *hupo*, it becomes *hupomone*, and it means *a person who is under a heavy load, but he has resolved that he's not moving*. It's like saying, "I don't care how heavy the load gets or how much pressure is put on me. I'm not budging. I'm not flinching. This is my territory. This is my promise. I'm not surrendering one inch of space." What a powerful word!

This word, *hupomone*, was used in a military sense to describe soldiers who were sticking it out. They outlasted all assaults and pressures and maintained their territory. All this meaning is in the word *hupomone*. A better translation would be *hang-in-there power*. This is what patience is: the ability to *hang in there, hold on, outlast*, and *persevere*.

In James 1:4, we read "…Let patience have her perfect work…." Interestingly, the word "patience" in Greek is feminine. We can think of patience like a woman who is pregnant. When she conceives, she doesn't give birth the next day. Imagine having a baby within 24 hours! If she did, her body and emotions wouldn't be ready, the room wouldn't be ready, nothing would be ready! Growth takes time. Preparation takes time. In the same way, patience requires time to complete its work in us.

Many times when we're asking God to do something in our lives or claiming the promises He made to us, we're doing everything correctly. We're believing in accordance with God's will. The promise is valid — yet we're not ready for the manifestation of that promise. The problem is never God. He is ready to give His promises to us right away, but *we* are not ready. It takes time for us to prepare to receive so that we can handle what God has said he's going to give us.

Rick shared an example of this on the program. When he and his wife Denise first got married, God spoke so clearly to Rick about their future that he knew with complete certainty all God had promised. Excited by these words, Rick tried to rush ahead and make those things happen immediately. But he just messed everything up. Why? He didn't yet have the maturity or experience to accommodate what God had promised.

Forty-five years later, Rick is seeing the manifestation of all those promises. What is the difference between those first attempts and now? This time, Rick is ready and prepared for them. He now has the experience to properly receive what God had promised, because **he had to grow into receiving them.**

Sometimes we're believing for things to take place in our lives, but we're not personally ready to accept what God wants to give us. So rather than say, *Why is God holding out on me?* It's better to take inventory of our lives and ask ourselves, *Am I doing what I need to do so that I can receive what God wants to promise and what God wants to give me?* It may not be the time for it just yet.

Looking again at James 1:4, it says, "But let patience have her perfect work...." You must let patience go to full term, just like a pregnant woman preparing for a baby. That way, you "may be perfect and entire, wanting nothing." To wholly grasp what is being said, let's look at the *Renner Interpretive Version (RIV)* of James 1:4:

> **But you're the one who must make the choice to let this God-given endurance do its work. And if you'll let endurance run its full course, it will advance you into higher levels of spiritual maturity. Choosing to let endurance run its full course takes**

work — but if you'll stick with this process all the way to the end, you'll advance to high spiritual levels in your life....

Isn't this interpretation powerful? So if it seems like God's promise is taking longer than expected to arrive, don't point your finger at God. Instead, ask yourself, *What is God preparing in me? What adjustments do I need to make so I can receive what He wants to give?* Maybe you need to make adjustments in your relationships or finances to accommodate what God wants to give you. Maybe it is something else entirely.

The creation of the *Renner Interpretive Version (RIV)* is another example of letting patience have its perfect work. For decades, it was on Rick's heart to compose the *Renner Interpretive Version*, but he had to wait until the time finally came for it to be developed and produced. The *Renner Interpretive Version (RIV)* is not a word-for-word translation, but a conceptual interpretation derived from the original Greek text. Rick's patience allowed the *RIV* to be born in the right season, and in 2025, he released the second installment of it.

This principle of timing is seen throughout Scripture — for example, in the life of Abraham. In Genesis 15, God promised Abraham that he would have a child. It took him 20 years to receive that promise, although he and Sarah probably could have received their promise much sooner. But Abraham was not ready for the manifestation of that promise. He kept messing up and doing things *his* way instead of *God's* way. So he had to grow into the promise before he could receive it. Isn't that encouraging? We can grow into receiving what God has promised to us.

So don't give up. Hold onto your faith and don't move from that position. Use that *hang-in-there power* and cling to the promise from God that you're believing for. You might not be ready for the manifestation of it just yet, but don't worry — you'll grow into the place of maturity where you can receive it. If you don't let go of His promise, it *will* come to pass.

Question Two: How do you know if you are moving out in "blind faith" to a land God will show you, like Abraham, or if you are trying to find God's promise in something He did not intend for you and you are making an "Ishmael decision"?

When you're considering taking a dramatic step of faith — something that is usually outside your comfort zone — you need multiple confirmations that what you are perceiving is correct. If you're married, you should have your spouse's confirmation also. Seek confirmation from godly, authoritative voices in your life. Proverbs 11:14 says, "Where no counsel is, the people fall: but in the multitude of counsellors there is safety." Listen to those with experience. Look for the green light in several areas before moving. Don't rush into a big step impulsively. But when the confirmations are clear and you have peace in your spirit, step through the door with confidence.

In the program, Rick shared a story from his own life about making an "Ishmael decision":

> I did an 'Ishmael' when I was young. I got offended with my pastor at the time, because he said, 'Rick, I know you're very impressed with yourself. But I want to tell you, you don't have the ability to go out and start a church on your own.' I didn't know I was impressed with myself, but those words offended me.
>
> In my state of offense, I thought I heard God say, 'Start a church.' But God did not say this — my flesh said it. I interpreted my offense as God speaking. I wanted to prove the pastor wrong, so I went out and started a church. It was small, and Denise and I were there for a couple of years. The people were precious but the church was never successful.
>
> And you know what? God is so good. He still blessed the people who came. People were saved, people were healed, and people were delivered. But I was not blessed. Why? Because God hadn't called me to start that church. I acted on my own. Today I call it *the Ishmael church*.

Rick's story illustrates what an Ishmael decision looks like. But here's the good news: Making a mistake does not mean everything is over. Abraham had been promised a child, but he tried to produce him in his own way — this is how Ishmael was born. It was a major mistake, yet Abraham wasn't discredited or cast aside. He still received God's promise — the right way — at the appointed time.

The same is true for you. If you've made a misstep, don't become so discouraged and think, *I'll never get it right. I'm going to quit trying.* Repent of the mistake and say, "Lord, let's do it Your way this time." You can move on from your mistake. This is what Abraham did. This is what Rick did. And this is what you can do too.

Question Three: Often, what God asks us to do can be scary or cause anxiety because it pushes the boundaries of our faith. How do we know the difference between something God is moving us toward for growth and something that we shouldn't do because we don't have peace on the inside?

Peace is very important. In fact, Colossians 3:15 tells us, "And let the peace of God rule in your hearts…." The word *rule* here literally means to act like an umpire, as in a baseball game. Peace in your heart lets you know if you are "safe" or "out." If you will listen to peace, you'll know when you're supposed to move forward and when you need to step back.

But here's the key: just because God asks you to do something new or something that stretches you, doesn't mean you'll feel perfectly comfortable. It's natural for you to have a little trepidation when He leads you beyond what you've known before. For example, when God told Joshua to lead the people of Israel across the Jordan, he said, "And it shall come to pass, as soon as the soles of the feet of the priests that bear the ark of the Lord, the Lord of all the earth, shall rest in the waters of Jordan, that the waters of Jordan shall be cut off from the waters that come down from above; and they shall stand upon an heap" (Joshua 3:13). The rest of the chapter reveals that the miracle didn't happen until they stepped into the water. Sometimes peace will show up as you move forward in obedience, and not before.

Rick experienced this himself when God called his family to move to Russia. His children were young, and it tested Rick's faith in following the Lord's leading and the peace in his heart. Many naysayers warned, "Don't go! You'll be moving into the land of communism." Everything about the move looked frightening. Yet in the core of his being, Rick knew God had spoken to him.

It was like the call of God to Abraham in Genesis 12, when God told him, "…Leave your native country, your relatives, and your family's family, and go to the land that I will show you" (Genesis 12:1 *NLT*). Abraham was the only one who heard that call, but he knew it was right and stepped out in faith. Rick did the same when God called him to Russia.

Rick also had people in his life whom he was in close relationship with who confirmed that what he was sensing was correct. His wife and children were in agreement. His pastor, Bob Yandian, said, "Rick, I just feel in my heart that you are right on track." That voice of spiritual authority mattered deeply to Rick. God can confirm His direction through pastors, sermons, and friends — but ultimately, you must know in your own heart that God is speaking to you.

At some point, you must stop praying about it and act on it. For Rick, that moment came on January 27, 1991, when he and his family boarded their flight to Russia. As soon as the engine roared and the plane took off, Rick heard God speak almost audibly to say, "Now your ministry begins." The confirmation from the Lord didn't come until he was already in motion. Likewise, when you step out to obey God, He will begin to speak to you.

When you obey God, you step into a life of adventure. If you've felt like you've been living in a black-and-white world, saying yes to God will open the door to a full spectrum of color and you'll experience life as you never have before.

Question Four: The Bible talks a lot about small beginnings and being faithful in the little things, but God always gives people assignments that are bigger than they are able to do on their own. How do you make progress to reach the vision?

The answer is simple: One step at a time. Zechariah 4:10 (*NLT*) says, "Do not despise these small beginnings, for the Lord rejoices to see the work begin...." God delights in small beginnings because He knows where they will lead. Every great vision He gives us starts small; not to discourage us, but to test our faithfulness and prepare us for more.

When Rick was a young man in 1977, the Holy Spirit spoke to him and said, "Write, write, write, and I'll prosper what you write." So Rick obeyed. He went straight to his keyboard and began to write. But he didn't start writing large, thick books right away. Rick began at the level he could — writing simple Gospel tracks and short leaflets. God was watching to see if he would be faithful. After that came his first book, *The Perfect Gift*, written when he was just 17 years old. It was never published, but the important part was that Rick was being obedient to the instruction of the Lord. Sometimes you don't know how to do everything God tells you to do, but you just have to start. Once you take the first step, God will show you the next one.

Another example of small beginnings is Rick's TV Ministry. Today, RENNER Ministries reaches multiple nations with the trusted teaching of the Bible through television, but that didn't happen overnight. Rick and his team prayed, sought wisdom, analyzed, and carefully considered each step. As they obeyed, one step at a time, God opened the door for the next step. And with each and every step, His provision came.

The same is true for you. If you're afraid to start small, you'll never get started at all, because everything begins small. And that's good news! Small beginnings allow you to grow, to develop, and to prepare your heart for the greater assignments God has planned. Every step of faith, no matter how small, moves you closer to the vision He has placed in your heart.

Question Five: What do you do if you know the call of God on your life, but it is a fight to see it come to pass?

When you know God's call on your life but find yourself in a fight to see it come to pass, the answer is clear: keep fighting. Paul wrote to Timothy to "fight the good fight of faith" (*see* 1 Timothy 6:12). But what exactly are you fighting? Often, the greatest battle is yourself. If you can overcome your own fears, doubts, and pride, you can overcome the devil and anything else that rises against you. You may have to battle fear of failure, fear of others' opinions, or the temptation to quit when progress seems slow. But you can win these battles, because you are an overcomer.

First John 5:4 (*AMP*) tells us, "For everyone born of God is victorious and overcomes the world; and this is the victory that has conquered and overcome the world — our [continuing, persistent] faith [in Jesus the Son of God]." That means the seed of victory is already inside you. God isn't asking you to have it all figured out — He is asking for your obedience. All He needs is your "yes." Once you decide to take that first step, He supplies the strength to keep moving forward.

So don't give up. Keep fighting, keep believing, and keep saying yes to God. The very fact that the fight is hard may be proof that your calling is worth it.

In the next lesson, we'll turn to another area of victory — what God's Word says about health and healing.

STUDY QUESTIONS

*Study to shew thyself approved unto God, a workman that
needeth not to be ashamed, rightly dividing the word of truth.*
— 2 Timothy 2:15

1. What does James 1:4 mean when it says, "let patience have her perfect work"? How does understanding the Greek word *hupomone* deepen your perspective on what it truly means to be patient?

2. How can making an "Ishmael decision" lead to unintended consequences? What biblical examples demonstrate the importance of waiting for God's timing? Consider Genesis 16:1-4, 21:1-2, and Ecclesiastes 3:1-13 as you reflect on this.

3. Why is peace in your heart a reliable indicator of God's guidance? (*See* Proverbs 3:5-6, Isaiah 26:3, and Colossians 3:15.) How were peace, personal conviction, and godly counsel, confirmations of God's will to Rick when he moved his family to Russia?

PRACTICAL APPLICATION

*But be ye doers of the word, and not hearers only,
deceiving your own selves.*
— James 1:22

1. In the program, Rick emphasized the importance of waiting for God's timing rather than rushing into decisions which could create an "Ishmael" in your life. In what areas of your life have you been tempted to act ahead of God's timing? How can you pause, seek confirmation from God, from wise counsel, and from the peace of the Holy Spirit before moving forward?

2. In this lesson, we learned the importance of sensing God's peace as an indicator of His guidance, just as Rick experienced before moving his family to Russia. How can you cultivate sensitivity to the peace of God in your decisions? Are there current decisions where you need to evaluate whether God's peace is present, and have you taken the initial step in faith to see God's guidance clearly?

3. Just as Rick started out writing tracts and leaflets before he could write books, identify one small task you can begin today that will prepare you for a larger vision God has given you. How will you remain

faithful in that small step, trusting that God will provide each next step as you walk in obedience?

TOPIC

Why Hasn't Your Healing Arrived?

SCRIPTURES

1. **Isaiah 53:5** — But he was wounded for our transgressions, he was bruised for our iniquities: the chastisement of our peace was upon him; and with his stripes we are healed.

2. **3 John 2** — Beloved, I wish above all things that thou mayest prosper and be in health, even as thy soul prospereth.

GREEK WORDS

No Greek words were shown on the TV program.

SYNOPSIS

Have you been praying, obeying God, and yet, still struggling with sickness in your body? If so, you're not alone. In this lesson, Rick reveals why healing sometimes seems delayed, how faith and practical action work together, and how you can pray effectively for yourself and others. Discover ways to stand strong in faith, support loved ones through health challenges, and trust God's perfect plan — even when healing doesn't happen on your timeline. Whether you're seeking physical, mental, or emotional wellness, this lesson will equip you to access the healing God has already provided.

The emphasis of this lesson:

Healing is a promise from God, but receiving it often involves cooperation between faith and action. In this lesson, Rick explores why sickness can persist despite prayer and obedience; how to pray for others; ways to support loved ones experiencing health challenges; and why some die while they are praying for healing. By understanding biblical principles,

taking practical steps for health, and standing on God's promises, believers can walk in both physical and spiritual wellness. Healing belongs to you, and through faith, diligence, and God's supernatural power, you can access all He has provided.

Question One: I've been obeying the Lord, and I have still been sick for years. What am I doing wrong? I have been praying and asking the Lord why and what I need to change. I'm doing everything that I can to obey the Lord.

If you've been faithfully following the Lord, praying, and obeying His Word, yet you're still struggling with sickness, it's not uncommon to wonder: *What am I doing wrong?* Many believers wrestle with this question. It can be frustrating and confusing when you're doing everything you know to do, yet healing seems delayed.

It's important to recognize that there are factors in our lives that can unintentionally hinder our healing. Understanding these can help you take the right steps forward. To address this topic in depth, Rick will release a new book titled *Everything You Need To Know About Healing* in early 2026. In it, he explains topics such as why Christians get sick, the price Jesus paid for healing, redemption's role in deliverance and healing, how to get well and stay well, the role of medicine and common sense, and how to stay strong and healthy as you grow older. He also addresses questions believers often ask, such as: *If Jesus died for our healing, why do some people still suffer and die?* By exploring what the Bible teaches about healing, you can gain clarity, strengthen your faith, and discover steps to receive the health God has promised. You can order this book by visiting our website at **renner.org**.

God *promised* healing to us. Isaiah 53:5 says, "…With his [Jesus'] stripes we are healed." What does this verse mean? Jesus died on the Cross for the forgiveness of sin — to release us from guilt and shame and to give us peace of mind. He also died for our physical healing. Some denominations claim this verse refers to spiritual healing, but that is not accurate. Scriptures show that physical and mental healing are what this verse is referring to.

Before we received Jesus, we were all spiritually dead. A dead man can't be healed; he can only be resurrected. So when people are born again, their spirits aren't *healed* — they're *resurrected*! First Peter 2:24 confirms what

Isaiah 53:5 says, showing that Jesus' death encompasses both mental and bodily restoration.

Yet it is possible to self-sabotage our healing. For instance, poor nutrition can lead to a whole horde of issues — high blood pressure, diabetes, or digestive issues, to name a few. Even if Jesus releases His power and healing manifests, unhealthy or wrong choices can allow sickness to return.

Stress, anxiety, worry, and fretfulness also negatively affect the body, opening the door for the devil to impact your health. Even though Jesus died for you to be well in your body and mind, if you're living in a state of anxiety and worry, those emotions can throw your body into a messy state and sabotage the healing that belongs to you.

Unforgiveness is another critical factor. Holding onto grudges or unresolved conflicts can create both emotional and physical strain. Individuals who practice forgiveness often experience better overall health. You can self-sabotage your healing by holding onto resentment, bad memories, or unforgiveness. And there are many, many more factors that go into your healing.

So when you're asking, "Why haven't I been healed even though I've been believing for it?" it's time to take a careful inventory. Examine your life and ask yourself:

- Are there areas where I have allowed the enemy to gain entry?
- Am I caring for my body properly?
- Am I holding onto unforgiveness or past hurts?
- Is worry dominating my life?
- How are my relationships affecting me?

Cooperating with God means taking practical steps as well as exercising your faith. If you want to be mobile, you need to move your body. Waiting passively for God to do everything without using common sense is unwise. People expect God to somehow magically make all things good without any effort on their side. Friend, you need to take care of your body and cooperate if you want to receive the manifestation of your healing.

Think of the steps you must take in maintaining a car. When you buy a brand-new car, you're proud of it. It sparkles, shines, and smells great. But as time goes by, you need to change the oil, fill the radiator, check the tires, and make other updates to keep it in good working condition.

What if you didn't do these things? What if you said, "I'm just going to believe and trust God that the oil will stay good forever"? Sitting back and expecting God to do all the work is foolish. Taking care of your car doesn't mean you lack faith — it means you're using common sense. In the same way, you need to exercise faith for God's healing while also taking action on the natural side of things.

Rick illustrated this principle with a real-life example. Many years ago, when RENNER Ministries built its large church building in Moscow — one of the finest Protestant church facilities in the country — it sparkled at the dedication. But maintaining that building requires continual effort, finances, and upkeep. Just as you wouldn't ignore your house, you can't ignore your body. Faith works best when paired with responsibility.

In the program, Rick shared a personal story about caring for one's body:

> Your body is your house. It's where you live, and just like any building, you've got to invest in it to keep it in pristine condition. You need to do more than just pray and believe that your body's going to stay in shape.
>
> I'm not speaking with any condemnation over anyone. Years ago, I was extremely overweight. I was so big, I was immobile. I just sat around all the time. I had to make a decision. I realized Jesus died for me to be healthy, and I'm only that size because I don't physically move. So I created a new lifestyle.
>
> I had people close to me hold me accountable to go to the gym, and I lost a hundred pounds. I still go regularly every single week. Not because I like to, but because I want my instrument, my body, to stay in good working condition. I know if I do my part while believing God for everything that belongs to me by redemption, then I'm working with God for my healing rather than believing and fighting Him at the same time.

The same principle applies in your own life. Whether restoring your body, nurturing relationships, or managing your home, faith without practical action is incomplete. Taking care of yourself — eating right, exercising, for-giving others, reducing stress, and building healthy relationships — allows the healing God has provided to not only manifest in your body, but to also *remain*.

This isn't all. We also need to know what the Word of God says and believe that it is true. Some people are sick because they're ignorant about what has been promised. For example, you can have money in the bank and live like a pauper if you don't know that the money is there.

Healing *belongs* to you! Do you know that it's available? Do you truly believe that you have a right to it? You can access it through prayer, the laying on of hands, being anointed with oil, and standing in faith as taught in James chapter 5. God has given clear instructions because He desires for you to be physically and mentally well. Partner your faith with practical action and watch the fullness of His promises unfold in your life.

Question Two: How do I pray for someone who is sick?

The Bible makes it very clear how we're to pray for the sick: we pray with faith. In Mark 16:18, Jesus promised that believers "…shall lay hands on the sick, and they shall recover." That means you already have access to this ability just the same as Jesus and Paul did, or even Rick.

One of the simplest and most powerful things you can do is to lay your hands on someone and pray in Jesus' name. Your hands are like conduits of God's healing power. The more often you do this, the more people you'll see receive a healing manifestation. But for that to happen, you have to take your hands out of your pockets and place them on people who need prayer. Stand on the promise of Mark 16:18. Step out and believe, saying to yourself: "This verse is talking about me. When I lay hands on the sick, they will recover."

However, it's also important to notice what else the verse actually says. It doesn't promise that people will *instantly* get well, but that they will *recover*. Recovery can be a process. When Rick prays for people, he often says, "From the moment I take my hands off of you, you're going to start getting better." He has had testimony after testimony of people who improved from that very moment.

So don't overcomplicate it. Pray with faith, lay your hands on the sick, and trust God's Word. Healing belongs to you, and you can be a part of ministering it to others.

Question Three: How can I help a family member or friend who is going through a health challenge?

That person needs help because sickness is a thief. Jesus said in John 10:10 that the devil comes "…to steal, and to kill, and to destroy…." And isn't that exactly what sickness does? It steals your time, your energy, your finances, and even your focus. It's a distraction from the life God intends for you to live.

Sometimes, though, our own choices can open the door to sickness. Rick shared that when he has overworked himself and pushed his body too far, it often shows up as a sore throat. He realized those moments aren't random — they were the result of his neglecting proper balance and not taking care of his body. In other words, he had opened the door.

That's an important perspective when helping someone else through their own health challenge. If you have a loved one who has been prayed for and is still struggling, it's worth gently and lovingly asking: "Is there any area of your life where the enemy might have been given an open door?" That question isn't meant to condemn, but to help that person see where a change may be needed. Maybe it's rest, maybe it's unforgiveness, maybe it's another area in his or her life causing healing to be hindered.

Alongside asking those questions, your role is to encourage and pray for him or her. People fighting sickness often feel discouraged, and they need someone to lift them up in love and remind them that God is still their Healer. Love that person enough to pray, encourage, and — when needed — remind him or her to close any doors to the enemy that sickness is trying to slip through. Only he or she has the authority to close that door.

Question Four: Why do some people die before their healing manifests?

No one is a stranger to experiencing effects from the death of someone they love. It is a part of life, but it can be especially hard to understand when someone we love dies before we see his or her healing manifest. Many believers find themselves asking, "Why did this happen? Why did they die?" The truth is, no one on this side of eternity has all the answers. Only Jesus knows the whole picture.

Rick shared a personal example to illustrate this. One of Denise's assistants, whom she loved dearly like a daughter, battled cancer and ultimately passed away. Everyone around her was standing in faith with her for healing. People asked, "Why? Why didn't God heal her?" Rick acknowledged, "I don't know the answer to that question, but you know who does? She does. She's now in the presence of the Lord and knows why she wasn't healed. And it wasn't because of God — Jesus paid the price on the Cross for every person to be healed."

The reality is that believers who pass away from sickness immediately experience the fulfillment of that healing. All pain, all infirmities, all diseases are left behind. While we may temporarily lose someone here, that person eternally wins there. In Christ, we all win in the end.

The Bible tells us in Third John 2, "Beloved, I wish above all things that thou mayest prosper and be in health, even as thy soul prospereth." Jesus paid a great price for our healing and that is echoed in the sentiment of John to his readers. Healing is an issue we all face at some point, whether for ourselves or someone we love. While we may not always understand the reasons why people don't obtain their healing, we know the problem is never with God. But we can stand on His promises, trust His faithfulness, and do our part to receive.

In the next lesson, we will explore the power we have in Christ to stand against the enemy's attacks and assignments.

STUDY QUESTIONS

Study to shew thyself approved unto God, a workman that needeth not to be ashamed, rightly dividing the word of truth.
— 2 Timothy 2:15

1. In the program, Rick gave examples of caring for the body (diet, exercise, rest, forgiveness) while trusting in God's supernatural power. Why is it important to balance faith with practical wisdom when it comes to health?

2. How do the following verses encourage believers to actively pray for the sick? Mark 6:5, 7:32; Luke 4:40, 13:13; Acts 9:17 and 28:8. What does the word "recover" in Mark 16:18 teach us about the process of healing?

3. Luke 16:10 (*AMPC*) says, "He who is faithful in a very little [thing] is faithful also in much, and he who is dishonest and unjust in a very little [thing] is dishonest and unjust also in much." How might this

principle apply to the way we care for our bodies? What does this reveal about the relationship between small, consistent choices and experiencing God's greater promises of healing and health?

PRACTICAL APPLICATION

**But be ye doers of the word, and not hearers only,
deceiving your own selves.**
— James 1:22

1. In the program, Rick compared maintaining your body to maintaining a car or a house. What practical changes could you make in your daily life — such as rest, diet, or stress management — that would help you better cooperate with God's healing power?

2. Have you ever hesitated to pray for someone's healing because you weren't sure of the results? How does Mark 16:18 challenge you to step out in faith, "get your hands out of your pockets," and be a conduit of God's healing power?

3. Supporting a loved one dealing with sickness often requires both compassion and candid conversation. Think of someone you know who is walking through a health challenge. What is one way you can encourage that person in faith, and one gentle, practical question you could ask to help him or her identify areas that may need to change?

LESSON 4

TOPIC

How Do You Walk in Authority?

SCRIPTURES

1. **2 Corinthians 10:4** — For the weapons of our warfare are not carnal, but mighty through God to the pulling down of strong holds.

2. **Luke 10:19** — Behold, I give unto you power to tread on serpents and scorpions, and over all the power of the enemy: and nothing shall by any means hurt you.

3. **2 Corinthians 12:7** — And lest I should be exalted above measure through the abundance of the revelations, there was given to me a

thorn in the flesh, the messenger of Satan to buffet me, lest I should be exalted above measure.

GREEK WORDS
No Greek words were shown on the TV program.

SYNOPSIS
Every battle you face begins in the mind. Lies appear that whisper you're not enough, you can't change, and your past will always define you. Left unchecked, those lies grow into strongholds — mental walls that shut out truth and imprison you in fear or limitation. But Scripture tells us we've been given mighty weapons to tear down those strongholds and walk in freedom.

In this lesson, you'll learn how to cast down imaginations that rise up against you, and how to stand in the authority Jesus has given you to prevail over the power of the enemy. We'll also look at questions regarding topics that have puzzled many believers, addressing matters such as generational curses and Paul's thorn in the flesh, and see how God's Word brings the answer with clarity and confidence. Life is not about barely surviving your struggles; it's about knowing who you are in Christ, exercising your God-given authority, and walking free in the grace and power that's already yours.

The emphasis of this lesson:

You are not powerless, for in Christ you have authority over every work of the enemy. Strongholds can be torn down and lies can be replaced with truth. Your family's past no longer defines you — you have been redeemed and set free. And when opposition rises against you, God's grace will always prove sufficient. Living in victory begins with renewing your mind to these truths and choosing to walk in them daily.

Question One: How do you practically cast down imaginations that exalt themselves against you?

Every battle you face in life is first fought in the arena of your thought life. The enemy knows that if he can plant a lie in your mind and let it grow, he can limit your faith, your peace, and even your health. That is why Paul told us in Second Corinthians 10:4-5 that we are not powerless in this fight — we've been given mighty weapons with the ability to pull down strongholds. Let's take a moment to look at this verse:

> **For the weapons of our warfare are not carnal, but mighty through God to the pulling down of strong holds; casting down imaginations….**
> — **2 Corinthians 10:4-5**

So what exactly is a stronghold? According to Scripture, a stronghold is a lie in the mind that dominates your thinking until your mind functions like a prison. In fact, the word "stronghold" in the Greek describes both *a castle* and *a prison*. Think of an old medieval castle. Each one has tall, thick, impenetrable walls built to keep enemies or intruders from getting inside. Meanwhile, a prison has the opposite purpose; it's designed to keep people on the inside from getting out. A mental stronghold does both — it shuts out the truth while trapping you inside a lie. Even though the people on the outside try to tell you the truth of your situation or belief, those truths don't penetrate or get through to you.

Rick once knew someone who believed nobody liked her and that she was "less than" everyone else. The truth was the exact opposite — she was full of life and fun. People enjoyed her. Yet she believed she was flawed and unworthy. No matter how often people told her differently, she couldn't accept it. That false belief became her prison.

That's how strongholds work. They convince you to live behind imaginary bars that feel just as real as steel. You find yourself looking out of those imaginary bars, wishing you could be like others, when in reality, you're just as valuable, capable, and gifted as they are.

Imagine someone with a remarkable singing gift, but who believes his talent is inferior to others. From behind those mental bars, he compares himself to others and wishes he had the vocals they have, not realizing his gift might actually surpass theirs. Because he believes the lie that he's not good enough, he hides his voice. His gift stays locked away, concealed because of his mental stronghold. And that gift never shines the way God intended it to. Wouldn't that be a sad waste of a God-given gift?

Rick had a similar experience which he shared on the program, about his own mental stronghold:

When I was a younger man, I lived with a horrible stronghold — I believed that I was stupid and inferior to others. I carried that every day. I would look in the mirror each morning and think, *Why do you exist? You don't deserve to exist.* I truly believed I was stupid.

In ninth grade I had a teacher named Mrs. Sparks who didn't like me or my family, so she nicknamed me 'Stupid.' Every day she called the roll and, when she came to my name, she'd say, 'Stupid Renner?' I was expected to answer, 'Here.' The other kids thought it was funny, and soon they were all calling me that too. I'd walk down the hall and hear, 'Hello, Stupid. Where are you going?' or, 'Stupid! How are you, Stupid?'

That experience was from the devil, trying to drive that belief into my mind: *You're stupid. You're inferior. There's something wrong with you.* That same year, the school gave job-placement tests which each student took to help determine his or her future career. A couple of weeks later, two counselors called me into the cafeteria to advise me about the results. I'll never forget what they said next. They looked at me and said, 'Ricky, we don't want to hurt you, but we need to tell you the truth. You do not have the mental stature to ever try any kind of higher education. You should never go to college. We wouldn't even encourage you to go to junior college based on your test results. We think that you need to think about doing something manual — dig ditches or help lay asphalt on the roads.'

There's nothing wrong with those jobs — we need people to do them — but those jobs weren't God's plan for me. It was a message from the devil who was trying to stop me before I ever got started. I really believe the devil knew what God was going to do with my life, and he was trying to suppress me from every side. He knew I was going to write books and that God was going to use me to touch the world. I heard the devil's lies in my head, I saw it in the mirror, and I heard it from my teacher, the kids, and even the counselors.

But everything changed in tenth grade when I received the baptism of the Holy Spirit. It was a lifesaver. When the power of God came on me, it broke the shackles around my mind.

Suddenly I could think clearly and see correctly. I began to see myself being used by God. It was like Clark Kent stepping into a phone booth and coming out as Superman. The Holy Spirit set me free.

That doesn't mean the lies never tried to come back. They did. When they do, you need to decide to pull them down and cast them out. In Greek, the words "pull down" or "cast down" mean *to disassemble piece by piece until nothing remains.*

I remember my dad once bought an old, dilapidated house in downtown Tulsa because he needed bricks to build a garage. Rather than buy new bricks, he said, 'Ricky, you and I are going downtown every day and we're going to disassemble that house, clean every brick, and take them home.' The first time he handed me a hammer, I looked at that house and thought, *You've got to be kidding me.* Yet brick by brick, we took that house apart. We'd knock one brick free, chip the mortar off, and set the clean brick aside. Piece by piece, we pulled that house down until there was nothing left.

We didn't just stand there and wish the house would fall. It took working with our own hands and personal effort. That's exactly what we must do with strongholds.

Similar to that old house Rick and his father pulled down, brick by brick, we need to do the same with the strongholds the devil tries to build in our minds. Second Corinthians 10:5 doesn't tell us to sit back and wish strongholds away — it says *to cast them down* or *to pull them down.*

If the enemy has solidified a lie in your thinking, it won't simply vanish on its own. *You* have to get involved. That means renewing your mind to the truth of God's Word. It means letting others speak truth into your life. It means opening your mouth and declaring the truth until, brick by brick, piece by piece, the lie is dismantled in your mind.

A stronghold is an attack against you — it's a mental prison that prevents you from knowing who you are in Christ, from walking in peace, and from fulfilling your calling. Don't stop until it is completely taken apart and you are free.

The reason many never achieve this kind of freedom is because they aren't fully committed to it. But make no mistake: the devil is very committed to your bondage. That's why you must be *more committed* to your freedom. Get involved in the process, stay consistent, and keep casting down every imagination until nothing remains. Rick is a living testimony that it can be done — and you can do it too! You can be completely free.

Question Two: How do Christians take authority over demonic activity?

When you became a Christian, you stepped onto a battlefield. The devil is real, and his goal is to steal, kill, and destroy (*see* John 10:10). But Jesus didn't leave us defenseless. Luke 10:19 said, "Behold, I give unto you power to tread on serpents and scorpions, and over all the power of the enemy: and nothing shall by any means hurt you." When Jesus sent His disciples out into the world, they faced dangerous conditions. In those days, roads were scarce and often full of holes and ruts. Snakes and scorpions would hide in those places, waiting to strike. Travelers were constantly afraid of being bitten or stung.

But Jesus gave them reassuring news: power was given to us by God! The word "behold" in Greek literally means *wow*. It's as if Jesus were saying, "Wow, listen to this! What I'm about to tell you is amazing." He then went on to say, "I give unto you *power*." That word "power" in the Greek means *authority*.

Jesus was saying, "I'm giving you authority to trample serpents and scorpions." In other words, you don't have to fear dangers in the natural world. If you're walking in God's will, you have authority even over the natural things that threaten you.

But Jesus doesn't stop there. He added, "…and over all the power of the enemy…" (Luke 10:19). The word "over" in Greek describes *a superior position*, and the word "all" is *all-inclusive, leaving nothing out*. That means you've been given authority over every single work of the devil — not just some of them, not just the small ones, but *all of them*.

Then Jesus makes the promise even stronger: "…and nothing shall by any means hurt you." In the Greek text, this phrase indicates three negatives in a row — *nothing, no, not* by any means. It's unusual grammar, but it's Jesus' way of underlining the truth: *Absolutely nothing at all will have the power to harm you.*

So what does this mean for you today? It means that Jesus has given you authority over both natural dangers and spiritual enemies. But to walk in that authority, you need to know who you are in Christ. You have to renew your mind to the truth of God's Word.

John 1:12 says, "But as many as received him, to them gave he power to become the sons of God...." The word "power" here is the Greek word *exousia*, which means *authority* and *influence*. The moment you became a child of God, you were given divine authority you never had before. All this is yours in Christ!

Question Three: What are your thoughts about generational curses?

Many people wonder if they're doomed to repeat the sins, struggles, or failures of their parents and grandparents. But here's the truth: **When you were born again, you received a great salvation.** Redemption in Christ isn't partial. It doesn't leave you chained to the failures of the past. Once you understand what redemption really means, you'll see that the power of Christ completely breaks the cycle of generational curses.

So what does redemption mean? It means Jesus purchased you out of the slave market of sin. The chains were broken off of you. According to Colossians 1:13, you were delivered out of the power of darkness and translated into the kingdom of God's Son where there are no curses.

You may still face hereditary *inclinations* to certain things. For example, your family may have a tendency toward alcoholism. Then you need to be aware of that and be responsible not to drink. Or your family may have a history of certain illnesses. If so, you need to use your faith to overcome them. But these are natural propensities rather than curses.

The good news is that it doesn't matter what's in your family lineage. First John 5:4 declares, "For whatsoever is born of God overcometh the world: and this is the victory that overcometh the world, even our faith." You have a faith that overrides every natural or spiritual tendency. So it doesn't matter what is in your family's past — by faith, you can override it all.

That's why it's vital to learn how to use your faith. Hebrews 2:3 tells us we have *a great salvation*. A great salvation is not one that leaves curses intact. No, when you were saved, you were delivered. The blood of Jesus broke every chain, including any generational curse that once tried to cling to your life. So embrace this truth: You've been freed. You've been unshackled. In Christ, every curse is broken.

Question Four: What was Paul's thorn in the flesh?

In Second Corinthians 12, Paul wrote about "a thorn in the flesh." Many people assumed this meant Paul struggled with sickness, but Paul never said that. Others think it referred to pride, but that really isn't what this means. So what was Paul actually describing? Let's look at what this verse actually says:

> **And lest I should be exalted above measure through the abundance of the revelations, there was given to me a thorn in the flesh, the messenger of Satan to buffet me, lest I should be exalted above measure.**
> **— 2 Corinthians 12:7**

Paul was essentially saying, "Because of the abundance of revelations God has given me, I'm making roads no one has ever made before. I'm preaching to people no one has ever reached. I'm speaking to kings and rulers. What is happening through me is amazing, and the devil wants to stop me."

The word "buffet" in this verse means *to beat with a fist, to try to stop*, and *to knock down*. The word "thorn" comes from a Greek word that describes *a stake on which one sticks a decapitated head*. Paul was saying, "The enemy is out for my head because of the revelations I've received." The devil doesn't just sit around and twiddle his thumbs. He assaults you to stop you from making significant advancements for the Kingdom of God.

So what was this thorn Paul was referring to? It wasn't sickness. It was people. The devil stirred up and used people to resist Paul everywhere he went. Read the book of Acts and you'll see it: mobs, riots, betrayals, imprisonment. Paul repeatedly faced people who tried to silence him and stop the furtherance of the Gospel.

That's why Paul said, "For this thing I besought the Lord thrice, that it might depart from me. And he said unto me, My grace is sufficient for thee: for my strength is made perfect in weakness..." (2 Corinthians 12:8-9). Paul had been asking God to remove the people opposing him, but that was a prayer God couldn't answer. Even if God removed one group, the devil would raise up another. Instead, God gave Paul the grace to overcome every attack, every opposition, every single time.

And that's the good news for you as well. When you face resistance, when people come against you because of your obedience to God, don't lose heart. You have access to the same grace Paul did. God's grace will empower you to stand firm, to keep going, and to finish the work He's called you to do.

In the next lesson, we'll take a closer look at questions about the Bible itself — why there are so many interpretations, which translations to trust, and how to approach the Scriptures with confidence.

STUDY QUESTIONS

Study to shew thyself approved unto God, a workman that needeth not to be ashamed, rightly dividing the word of truth.
— 2 Timothy 2:15

1. Second Corinthians 10:3-5 (*AMPC*) says, "For though we walk (live) in the flesh, we are not carrying on our warfare according to the flesh and using mere human weapons. For the weapons of our warfare are not physical [weapons of flesh and blood], but they are mighty before God for the overthrow and destruction of strongholds, [inasmuch as we] refute arguments and theories and reasonings and every proud and lofty thing that sets itself up against the [true] knowledge of God; and we lead every thought and purpose away captive into the obedience of Christ (the Messiah, the Anointed One)." According to this passage and what you have learned in this lesson, what does it mean to "pull down strongholds"? How does understanding this change the way you think about challenges or opposition you are confronted with?

2. Colossians 1:13 says we were delivered out of the power of darkness and translated into the kingdom of God's Son. How does this verse explain what Christ has accomplished for us regarding redemption? What specific areas of life does this redemption cover?

3. Read the following Scriptures to reinforce your understanding of the authority you have in Christ over the enemy: Matthew 28:18-20; Mark 16:17-18; Luke 10:19; Romans 16:20; Ephesians 6:10-18; Colossians 2:15; James 4:7; and First John 4:4. What do these passages

teach about the relationship between Christ's power and our authority as His followers? What patterns or themes do you notice across these scriptures about the believer's position over the enemy?

PRACTICAL APPLICATION

But be ye doers of the word, and not hearers only, deceiving your own selves.
— James 1:22

1. A stronghold is a lie in the mind that dominates your thinking until your mind functions like a prison. That stronghold works against your calling, your peace, and your identity in Christ. The devil is committed to your bondage, so you must be *even more* committed to your freedom. Are you truly committed to walking in freedom? What recurring lie or "stronghold" have you struggled with, and what practical steps can you take this week to replace it with God's truth?

2. Consider your family history. Are there any patterns, fears, or behaviors that have seemed to have a generational root? If so, how does Christ's redemption reshape the way you view those patterns, and what choices can you make today to walk in the freedom He provides?

3. In Romans 12:2, Paul urged us to be transformed by the renewing of our minds. How does this practice help us to walk daily in victory? What specific actions can you take to intentionally renew your mind each day — using Scripture, prayer, worship, or another method — so that God's truth remains at the forefront of your thoughts?

LESSON 5

TOPIC
What Issues Are Worth Debating?

SCRIPTURES

1. **1 Corinthians 14:33-35** — For God is not the author of confusion, but of peace, as in all churches of the saints. Let your women keep silence in the churches: for it is not permitted unto them to speak; but they are commanded to be under obedience as also saith the law. And

if they will learn any thing, let them ask their husbands at home: for it is a shame for women to speak in the church.

2. **Hebrews 6:1** — Therefore leaving the principles of the doctrine of Christ, let us go on unto perfection; not laying again the foundation of repentance from dead works, and of faith toward God.

GREEK WORDS

No Greek words were shown on the TV program.

SYNOPSIS

Faith thrives when it is built on a strong foundation of truth. Yet throughout history, believers have wrestled with countless questions about Scripture, doctrine, and how to live out their faith in a world full of competing voices. In this lesson, Rick addresses some of the most practical and sometimes controversial questions Christians face today: Why are there so many Bible translations? Can women preach in church? How should we handle differences of opinion with family members? What does true surrender look like? And what are the foundational doctrines every believer must know? Through biblical teaching and real-life wisdom, Rick answers these questions, reminding us that clarity comes from God's Word and stability comes from building our lives on it with Christ as our foundation.

The emphasis of this lesson:

God desires His people to be firmly grounded in His Word, able to discern truth from error, and to live with wisdom, humility, and strength. By exploring questions about Bible translations, the role of women in the ministry, choosing a church, handling family disagreements, continual surrender, and the elementary doctrines of faith, we learn that the Christian life is both practical and deeply spiritual. When we build on the right foundation, our faith stands strong, and we are equipped to live boldly, love well, and remain steadfast in Christ.

Question One: Why are there so many interpretations of the Bible?

The original text of the Bible was primarily written in Hebrew and Greek. For example, the New Testament was written in Greek, and unless you can read Greek, you need a translation or an interpretation to read it. There are multiple translations and interpretations available today, and many of them are wonderful tools for understanding God's Word. However, it's important to remember that language evolves.

Take James 2:2-3, for instance, where the *King James Version* says, "For if there come unto your assembly a man...that weareth the *gay* clothing...." The word "gay" doesn't carry the same meaning as it did 300 years ago. Back then, it simply meant bright or colorful clothing. Today the meaning of that word has completely changed, requiring a modern translation or interpretation to convey the original intent accurately. While languages and words change, the original text never does.

The first major translation of the Old Testament was the Septuagint — the Greek translation of the Hebrew Scriptures. By 200 B.C., following the conquest of Alexander the Great, Greek had become the dominant language across much of the eastern world, including in Israel. Hebrew was primarily reserved for scholars, while the common people spoke Greek and Aramaic. When Jesus read from the scrolls in the synagogue, it is believed He read from the Septuagint, which was widely used throughout Israel at the time. Translation, then, is not a new concept.

Later, Jerome became the first to translate the Bible into Latin, producing what is known as the Vulgate over a period of 23 years — all while living in a grotto near Bethlehem, which was part of the Church of the Holy Nativity. Jerome's translation became the standard for more than a thousand years and influenced countless subsequent translators, including Martin Luther and John Wycliffe. Each translator built on the work of those who came before, refining and expanding the reach of God's Word. Even the *King James Version*, which some people insist is the only translation you should read, acknowledges in its introduction the debt the translators felt to those who came before them, expressing gratitude for previous translations and the work of earlier scholars.

Today, new translations and interpretations continue this tradition, including Rick's own *Renner Interpretive Version* (*RIV*), which focuses on a conceptual interpretation of the Greek text to capture nuance and meaning. Translation is a labor of love, requiring thousands of hours of careful work, and we benefit immensely from the dedication of those who devote their lives to bringing Scripture to us in ways we can understand.

Question Two: Is there one translation of the Bible that is superior to the rest?

In Rick's opinion, there are no translations that are inherently superior to the rest. He uses many translations and appreciates each for different reasons. He does have favorites, such as the *New Living Translation* and, of course, the *King James Version*. While the *King James Version* is his all-time favorite, it's not because it is the most accurate. Rather, it is the version he used when he began to study the Word of God as he was growing up and it's easy to memorize.

A helpful way to study Scripture is to compare multiple translations. Websites like **Biblehub.com** make this easy, allowing you to explore various translations and interpretations. Make it a habit to read Scripture through multiple lenses and notice how God uses different translations to speak to you in fresh ways.

Question Three: I've never quite understood the command for women to stay silent in church, even to ask a question. Why does it only apply to women and not men?

This is a question that often causes confusion, but understanding the historical and cultural context helps us see Paul's intention more clearly. Let's look at the verse in First Corinthians 14 to understand what he was addressing:

> **For God is not the author of confusion, but of peace, as in all churches of the saints. Let your women keep silence in the churches: for it is not permitted unto them to speak; but they are commanded to be under obedience as also saith the law. And if they will learn any thing, let them ask their husbands at home: for it is a shame for women to speak in the church.**
> **— 1 Corinthians 14:33-35**

Some believe this verse restricts women from speaking or taking any public role in the Church. They conclude that women can't preach and must remain silent. This is an incomplete understanding. When we examine Scripture as a whole, we see that Paul worked with women who actively taught and preached. For instance, Priscilla played a crucial role in instructing Apollos so that he would teach the Word of God accurately (*see* Acts 18:24-28). In fact, Romans 16 suggests she may have even had an apostolic calling. Clearly, women served in public ministry roles alongside men.

So why did Paul write that women should be silent in church? To understand this, we have to look at the cultural context of the time. Men and women were largely separated in public spaces. Women were typically not allowed to shop or participate in public meetings; men handled all public affairs. The marketplace was only for men, as men did all the shopping. If a woman was seen in the marketplace, she was usually a prostitute standing in a corner. Women were rarely seen outside their homes, and men and women didn't even sit together in public meetings.

The very fact that Paul addressed women in church was revolutionary — it meant women were now participating in public meetings and worship with men, something previously unheard of! This was only made possible through Christ. Galatians 3:28 says, "…There is neither male nor female: for ye are all one in Christ Jesus."

When Paul said, "Let your women keep silence…," he was addressing a brand-new situation: women were now participating in public gatherings alongside men. His instruction wasn't meant to suppress women, but to guide them in proper etiquette for this new, unprecedented setting. During church gatherings, women asked questions and spoke loudly to their husbands for clarification. They wanted to learn!

Paul was not against women in the church. He wasn't even against women asking questions. Paul's point was not to prevent learning but to maintain order in the service, so questions and discussion should happen at home afterward, not during the meeting. Women were learning how to participate appropriately in a new, mixed-gender context.

Similarly, in First Timothy 2:11-12, Paul instructed that women should not exercise authority in a service in ways not given to them. Yet the same standard applies to men — no one should take authority inappropriately during a service. The principle is about maintaining proper order, not about restricting women based on gender.

Question Four: Is it okay for women to preach in church?

Women are absolutely allowed to preach. If they are called and recognized by church authority, they can do everything a man can do in ministry. Rick mentioned that he and Denise grew up in a denomination where women were not allowed to preach, yet women could do almost everything else. They could teach Sunday school, serve as missionaries, and even lead mission initiatives. For example, Rick's church had two major mission offerings each year — one was in honor of Lottie Moon, and the other was in honor of Annie Armstrong, women who both dedicated their lives to the mission field. Yet, despite their active service, women were not permitted to preach in the church. It was such a clear contradiction! They could go overseas and give their lives in ministry, but they couldn't preach in their own country.

This thinking doesn't align with the New Testament. God pours out of His Spirit on both men *and* women (*see* Acts 2:17-18). In Romans 16, we see women recognized among the apostles, some with pastoral authority. The example of Aquila and Priscilla illustrates this clearly — Priscilla was highly anointed and acknowledged as a teacher, and First Corinthians 16:19 reveals that she and her husband even had a church that met in their house. Priscilla's impact was so significant that some have even speculated — though we can't know for certain — that she may have written the book of Hebrews. While this is unconfirmed, it demonstrates the tremendous influence Priscilla had in the early ministry of the Church, teaching and preaching with authority.

Because God pours out of His Spirit on *all* flesh, women can be powerfully anointed teachers and preachers, just like men!

Question Five: I've moved to a new city for work, and I'm looking for a church. I've tried a few, but none of them feels like the right place. I know it's important to attend church, so should I just pick one based on its alignment with my beliefs?

Church should be your top priority. Ideally, you would research churches before moving to a new city, because Scripture commands us not to forsake the assembling of ourselves together (*see* Hebrews 10:25). But if you've already moved and are visiting churches without finding one that speaks to you, focus on finding a church that aligns with you spiritually and doctrinally, led by a pastor with integrity.

Remember, no church is perfect. If you're expecting perfection, you'll likely be disappointed. Instead, listen to the leading of the Holy Spirit, select the church that best aligns with your beliefs, and give it your full support. Serve with a joyful heart, help the church financially by giving tithes and offerings, and commit to being an active member. Your dedication, even in an imperfect church, will allow you to grow and flourish in your faith.

Question Six: What is the best way to respectfully express a differing theological perspective to a family member?

Sometimes the best way to handle a differing theological perspective is not to express it at all. We all have family members who believe differently, and that's okay. As Rick shared in the program, "If I know that what I'm about to say is going to be a strife-filled issue — unless I know I'm going to make a difference — I'm not going to bring it up. I will probably ignore the topic unless I know I can say something that will really help someone."

The book of Proverbs reminds us, "In the multitude of words sin is not lacking, but he who restrains his lips is wise" (Proverbs 10:19 *NKJV*). Sometimes it's far better to be quiet than to speak. If you know a conversation will only stir up strife or division, why bring it up? Unless you truly feel led by the Holy Spirit that your words will help that person, it's often best to let it go. It's okay to have different opinions, and it's okay to not always voice yours.

Question Seven: When we surrender something to the Lord, is it truly surrendered if we keep bringing it up to Him?

Surrender is central to walking with Christ. Rick reflected on his salvation story while answering this question. At just five years old, he walked down to the front of the church while the song "I Surrender All" played overhead. He remembers thinking, "All to Jesus I surrender, all to Him I freely give, I will ever love and trust Him." That day, Rick called on Jesus as the Lord of his life and surrendered himself fully to Him.

Rick has been surrendering ever since. Every morning when he wakes up, he re-surrenders. There's nothing wrong with that. In fact, Scripture calls us to "live" at the altar, as living sacrifices before God (*see* Romans 12:1). That's the picture of *continual* surrender.

So is it wrong if you keep surrendering the same thing? Not at all. Each day is a new opportunity to reaffirm your trust in Him. True surrender isn't about never mentioning something again — it's about continually yielding your heart and will to God.

Question Eight: What are the elementary ABCs of the Christian faith, and why are they so important?

If you don't have the right foundation, you will probably build a crooked building. Rick illustrated this with a story about a city in the former Soviet Union, where architects raced to prove they could build a skyscraper faster than anyone else. They succeeded, but the foundation was flawed. Today that massive structure still stands on the banks of a river, leaning so badly that it can't be occupied. Instead, it's used only for advertising.

The same is true spiritually — if you want to build a lasting life of faith, you must start with the right foundation. Hebrews 6 lays out what Rick calls the "elementary ABCs" of our faith:

- Repentance from dead works
- Faith toward God
- The doctrine of baptisms
- The laying on of hands
- The resurrection of the dead
- Eternal judgment

These are the foundation stones of our Christian faith. If even one of them is misaligned, your "building" can lean off balance. But when they're in place, you can build a strong spiritual superstructure that will last.

Rick has written a book called *Build Your Foundation* that explores each of these doctrines in detail — what they mean, why they matter, and how to make sure they're solid in your life. You can order a copy of it by visiting our website at **renner.org/store**.

Over the course of this study, we've explored questions about the end times and the Rapture, how to follow God's guidance and timing in our lives, what His Word says about health and healing, the authority we have over the enemy, and the importance of living surrendered and grounded in the foundational truths of the faith. Each of these truths builds upon the other, giving us a strong, steady foundation for our walk with Christ.

As you move forward, remember to keep returning to God's Word, applying what you've learned, and allowing the Holy Spirit to strengthen you daily. The more you walk in these truths, the more unshakable your life will become, firmly built on Christ, our Cornerstone and foundation.

STUDY QUESTIONS

Study to shew thyself approved unto God, a workman that
needeth not to be ashamed, rightly dividing the word of truth.
— 2 Timothy 2:15

1. In the program, Rick shared that many people are confused about why there are so many translations of the Bible. After hearing his explanation, what stood out to you about the value of different translations? How does Hebrews 4:12 remind us that the power is not in the style of translation but in the living Word of God itself?

2. The role of women in ministry has been debated for centuries. What passages of Scripture help shed light on women being used by God in teaching, leadership, and ministry (*consider* Acts 18:24-26 and Romans 16:1-7)? How does Rick's explanation bring clarity to this sometimes controversial subject?

3. Hebrews 6:1-2 lists the elementary "ABCs" of the Christian faith — repentance from dead works, faith toward God, baptisms, laying on of hands, resurrection of the dead, and eternal judgment. Why are these called the foundations? How might misunderstanding or neglecting even one of these affect a believer's walk with God?

PRACTICAL APPLICATION

But be ye doers of the word, and not hearers only,
deceiving your own selves.
— James 1:22

1. Think about your personal Bible reading. Do you feel limited to one translation, or do you allow different translations to give you a fresh perspective on Scripture? This week, try comparing the same passage in two translations and note how it deepens your understanding.

2. Have you ever found yourself in conflict with a family member or another believer over a spiritual matter? If you have, reflecting on the situation, did you approach it with humility and grace, or with pride and frustration? What principle in Romans 14 can you apply in your relationships about this subject moving forward?

3. Surrender is not a moment but a lifestyle. What area of your life do you sense God asking you to freshly yield to Him right now? Write it

down and pray daily this week, asking God for strength to release it into His hands.

4. Out of the six foundational doctrines in Hebrews 6, which one do you feel the most confident about understanding, and which one do you feel the least confident about? How could you take one practical step to grow deeper in that area?

A Prayer To Receive Salvation

If you've never received Jesus as your Savior and Lord, now is the time for you to experience the new life Jesus wants to give you! To receive God's gift of salvation that can be obtained through Jesus alone, pray this prayer from your heart:

Jesus, I repent of my sin and receive You as my Savior and Lord. Wash away my sin with Your precious blood and make me completely new. I thank You that my sin is removed, and Satan no longer has any right to lay claim on me. Through Your empowering grace, I faithfully promise that I will serve You as my Lord for the rest of my life.

If you just prayed this prayer of salvation, you are born again! You are a brand-new creation in Christ! Would you please let us know of your decision by going to **renner.org/salvation**? We would love to connect with you and pray for you as you begin your new life in Christ.

Scriptures for further study: John 3:16; John 14:6; Acts 4:12; Ephesians 1:7; Hebrews 10:19,20; 1 Peter 1:18,19; Romans 10:9,10; Colossians 1:13; 2 Corinthians 5:17; Romans 6:4; 1 Peter 1:3

Notes

Notes

CLAIM YOUR FREE RESOURCE!

As a way of introducing you further to the teaching ministry of Rick Renner, we would like to send you FREE of charge his teaching, "How To Receive a Miraculous Touch From God" on CD or as an MP3 download.

In His earthly ministry, Jesus commonly healed *all* who were sick of *all* their diseases. In this profound message, learn about the manifold dimensions of Christ's wisdom, goodness, power, and love toward all humanity who came to Him in faith with their needs.

☑ **YES, I want to receive Rick Renner's monthly teaching letter!**

Simply scan the QR code to claim this resource or go to:
renner.org/claim-your-free-offer

Connect

WITH US!

R renner.org

f facebook.com/rickrenner • facebook.com/rennerdenise

▶ youtube.com/rennerministries • youtube.com/deniserenner

instagram.com/rickrrenner • instagram.com/rennerministries_
instagram.com/rennerdenise

Dear Friend,

If you enjoyed this study guide and believe others would benefit from reading it, please leave a review on Amazon and recommend it to others — or *consider sharing a copy with a friend or loved one!*

There is a great need for *"teaching you can trust"* among God's people.

Your friends in Christ and for His Gospel,

www.ingramcontent.com/pod-product-compliance
Lightning Source LLC
Chambersburg PA
CBHW071644040426
42452CB00009B/1760

www.ingramcontent.com/pod-product-compliance
Lightning Source LLC
Chambersburg PA
CBHW071644040426
42452CB00009B/1760